THE GLOBAL FREELANCER

Finding Clients and Projects Anywhere

Genevieve Velzian

Copyright © 2024 Genevieve Velzian

All rights reserved

Please note that all recommendations made in this book are based on the aiuthor's own opinion and in no way represent legal advice. Please seek your own legal counsel. The author accepts no liability.

No part of this book may be reproduced, or stored in a retrieval system, or transmitted in any form or by any means, electronic, mechanical, photocopying, recording, or otherwise, without express written permission of the publisher.

CONTENTS

Copyright 3
Introduction 3
How to Come Up with Your Company Name as a Freelancer 3
Preparing for Global Freelancing 3
Creating Your Freelance Website 3
Finding Clients 3
Marketing Yourself 3
Marketing Your Business and Winning Clients 3
Managing International Projects 3
Legal and Financial Considerations 3
Building Long-Term Client Relationships 3
The Best Countries to Freelance From 3
Twenty Ideas for Freelance Businesses 3
How to Charge for Your Time as a Freelancer 3
Overcoming Loneliness as a Freelancer 3
Scaling Your Freelance Business 3
Maintaining Good Client Relationships as a Freelancer 3
Case Studies and Success Stories 3
The Future of Global Freelancing 3
The End 3
About The Author 3
Title Page 1

INTRODUCTION

Overview of Freelancing

Freelancing, once a niche domain for creative professionals and specialists, has evolved into a mainstream career choice. The term "freelancer" dates back to the early 19th century, originally referring to medieval mercenaries who offered their services to the highest bidder.

Today, it encompasses a vast array of professions—from writers and designers to software developers and consultants—reflecting the diverse opportunities available in the gig economy.

The rise of the gig economy has fundamentally transformed the employment landscape. Advances in technology, particularly the internet and digital communication tools, have enabled individuals to work independently from virtually anywhere.

This flexibility, coupled with the desire for a better work-life balance, has driven millions to pursue freelancing as a viable career path. As of the latest statistics, nearly 59 million Americans freelanced in 2020, and this number is expected to grow significantly in the coming years.

Purpose of the Book

Welcome to "The Global Freelancer: Finding Clients and Projects Anywhere." This book is your comprehensive guide to navigating the world of freelancing on a global scale. Whether you are a seasoned freelancer looking to expand your client base internationally or a newcomer seeking to break into the freelance market, this book will equip you with the knowledge and tools needed to succeed.

In the following chapters, you will learn how to prepare for global freelancing, find and attract clients, market yourself effectively, manage international projects, and build long-term client relationships.

You will also gain insights into the legal and financial aspects of freelancing, as well as strategies for scaling your business. Through case studies and success stories, you will see real-world examples of how freelancers have achieved their goals and overcome challenges.

The Global Freelancing Landscape

The global freelancing landscape is vast and dynamic, shaped by technological advancements, economic shifts, and changing work preferences. Here are some key trends and statistics that highlight the current state of global freelancing:

Remote Work Revolution: The COVID-19 pandemic accelerated the adoption of remote work, making it a standard practice for many companies and freelancers. This shift has opened up new opportunities for freelancers to work with clients from around the world without geographical constraints.

Diverse Opportunities: Freelancing is no longer limited to traditional fields like writing and graphic design. Today, freelancers can find opportunities in software development, digital marketing, virtual assistance, consulting, and more. Specialized skills are in high demand, allowing freelancers to command premium rates.

Freelance Platforms: Online platforms such as Upwork, Fiverr, Freelancer, and Toptal have become essential tools for freelancers to connect with clients globally. These platforms offer a wide range of projects, from short-term gigs to long-term contracts, catering to various skill levels and industries.

Economic Impact: The freelance economy contributes significantly to global GDP. In the United States alone, freelancers contributed approximately $1.2 trillion to the economy in 2020. As more individuals embrace freelancing, its economic impact is expected to grow.

Flexibility and Autonomy: One of the primary motivations for freelancing is the desire for greater flexibility and autonomy. Freelancers can choose their projects, set their schedules, and work from anywhere, providing a level of freedom that traditional employment often lacks.

While freelancing offers numerous benefits, it also presents challenges. Freelancers must navigate issues such as inconsistent income, lack of benefits, and the need for self-discipline. Additionally, working with international clients introduces complexities related to time zones, cultural differences, and legal considerations. This book will address these challenges and provide practical solutions to help you thrive as a global freelancer.

In summary, freelancing has become a powerful force in the modern economy, offering unparalleled opportunities for individuals to work independently and connect with clients worldwide.

"The Global Freelancer: Finding Clients and Projects Anywhere" will guide you through the intricacies of this dynamic field, equipping you with the strategies and insights needed to succeed.

Whether you are just starting your freelance journey or looking to take your business to the next level, this book is your essential companion in the global freelancing landscape.

HOW TO COME UP WITH YOUR COMPANY NAME AS A FREELANCER

Introduction

Choosing the right name for your freelance business is a crucial step in establishing your brand identity. A good company name can set you apart from the competition, convey your values, and make a lasting impression on potential clients. This chapter will guide you through the process of creating a memorable and effective company name for your freelance business.

Step 1: Define Your Brand Identity

Understand Your Values and Mission:

Reflect on your core values, mission, and the unique value you offer. Your company name should align with these elements.

Consider the message you want to convey to your clients. Are you aiming for professionalism, creativity, reliability, or innovation?

Identify Your Target Audience:

Think about who your ideal clients are and what they value. Your company name should resonate with them and attract their attention.

Consider the industry you are targeting and the language or tone that appeals to that market.

Step 2: Brainstorm Keywords and Ideas

List Relevant Keywords:

Write down keywords related to your services, skills, industry, and values. These keywords can serve as inspiration for your company name.

Include words that describe the benefits and outcomes of your work, such as "innovative," "creative," "efficient," or "trustworthy."

Use Creative Techniques:

Mind Mapping: Create a mind map with your core keywords and expand on related ideas and concepts.

Word Combinations: Experiment with combining different words and phrases. Consider blending parts of words or using alliteration for a catchy effect.

Synonyms and Thesaurus: Use a thesaurus to find synonyms for your keywords and explore different variations.

Step 3: Consider Different Naming Styles

Descriptive Names:

Clearly describe what your business does. These names are straightforward and easy to understand (e.g., "Smith Graphic Design," "Tech Solutions Consulting").

Invented Names:

Create a unique and original name that doesn't have a specific meaning but sounds appealing and memorable (e.g., "Zylo," "Novatek").

Compound Names:

Combine two or more words to create a new name that conveys a specific meaning (e.g., "WebCraft," "EcoMedia").

Acronyms:

Use the initial letters of a longer phrase or description to create a short, catchy name (e.g., "B2B Solutions," "SMM Experts").

Metaphorical Names:

Use metaphors or symbols that represent your business values or services (e.g., "Phoenix Marketing," "Lionheart Consulting").

Step 4: Ensure Uniqueness and Availability

Check Domain Availability:

Ensure that the domain name for your chosen company name is available. Use domain search tools like GoDaddy, Namecheap, or Bluehost to check availability.

Aim for a .com domain if possible, as it is the most recognized and trusted extension.

Search for Trademarks:

Conduct a trademark search to ensure that your chosen name is not already in use or protected by another business. Use tools like the USPTO's Trademark Electronic Search System (TESS) or international trademark databases.

Check Social Media Handles:

Verify that your chosen company name is available on major social media platforms like Twitter, Facebook, LinkedIn, and Instagram. Consistent branding across all platforms is important.

Avoid Confusing Similarities:

Ensure your name is distinct and not easily confused with existing brands or competitors. This helps avoid legal issues and builds a unique identity.

Step 5: Test Your Name

Get Feedback:

Share your top name choices with friends, family, and colleagues. Gather feedback on how the names are perceived and if they convey the intended message. Consider asking your target audience for their opinions through surveys or focus groups.

Visualize Your Name:

Create mockups of your company name in logos, business cards, and website headers. This helps you see how the name works in different contexts and if it fits your brand image.

Say It Out Loud:

Pronounce your chosen name out loud to ensure it sounds good and is easy to say. Avoid names that are difficult to pronounce or spell.

Step 6: Finalize and Register Your Name

Make Your Decision:

Based on feedback and testing, choose the name that best represents your brand and resonates with your target audience.

Register Your Domain and Social Media Handles:

Secure your domain name and create social media profiles using your chosen name to establish your online presence.

Legal Registration:

Register your business name with the appropriate government authorities. This process varies by country, so check the requirements for your location.

Trademark Your Name:

If your budget allows, consider trademarking your company name to protect it legally and prevent others from using it.

Conclusion

Choosing the right name for your freelance business is a crucial step in building a strong brand identity. By defining your brand values, brainstorming keywords, considering different naming styles, ensuring uniqueness, testing your name, and finally registering it, you can create a memorable and effective company name that resonates with your target audience and sets you apart from the competition.

Take the time to choose a name that reflects your vision and aspirations, and it will serve as a strong foundation for your freelance business.

This chapter on coming up with your company name as a freelancer provides a structured approach to finding the perfect name that aligns with your brand and appeals to your clients. A well-chosen name can enhance your professional image and contribute to your success in the freelancing world. Happy naming!

PREPARING FOR GLOBAL FREELANCING

Skills Assessment

Before diving into the global freelancing market, it's essential to assess your skills and identify those that are in demand. Start by listing your core competencies, including technical abilities, soft skills, and any specialized knowledge. Consider the following steps:

Identify Your Marketable Skills:

Technical Skills: These might include programming languages, graphic design, writing, digital marketing, or any specific expertise relevant to your field.

Soft Skills: Communication, time management, problem-solving, and adaptability are crucial for working with international clients.

Specialized Knowledge: Industry-specific knowledge or certifications can set you apart from other freelancers.

Benchmark Your Skills:

Research: Look at job postings and freelance profiles in your industry to understand the skills and qualifications that are in demand.

Self-Evaluation: Honestly evaluate your strengths and areas for improvement. Consider feedback from previous clients or employers.

Upskill and Get Certified:

Online Courses: Platforms like Coursera, Udemy, and LinkedIn Learning offer courses that can enhance your skills.

Certifications: Obtain certifications that are recognized globally, such as PMP for project management or Google Analytics for digital marketing.

Building Your Portfolio

A compelling portfolio is crucial for attracting clients. It showcases your skills, experience, and the quality of your work. Here's how to create an effective portfolio:

Select Your Best Work:

Quality Over Quantity: Choose projects that best demonstrate your skills and versatility.

Relevance: Include work that aligns with the type of projects you want to attract.

Showcase Your Work Effectively:

Detailed Descriptions: Provide context for each project. Explain your role, the challenges you faced, and the solutions you provided.

Visuals: Use images, screenshots, or videos to make your portfolio visually appealing.

Results: Highlight the outcomes of your work, such as increased traffic, higher sales, or improved efficiency.

Create a Professional Presentation:

Website: Consider creating a personal website to host your portfolio. Platforms like WordPress, Wix, and Squarespace make this easy.

PDF Portfolio: Have a well-designed PDF version that you can share with potential clients who prefer offline review.

Setting Up Your Online Presence

Having a strong online presence is essential for global freelancers. It helps potential clients find you and builds your credibility.

Website and Blog:

Personal Website: Your website should include your portfolio, a bio, services offered, client testimonials, and contact information.

Blog: Regularly update your blog with industry insights, case studies, and tips. This demonstrates your expertise and helps with SEO.

Social Media and Professional Networks:

LinkedIn: Optimize your LinkedIn profile with a professional photo, detailed work history, and endorsements. Join relevant groups and participate in discussions.

Other Platforms: Depending on your industry, consider using Twitter, Instagram, or Behance to showcase your work and connect with potential clients.

Online Communities: Participate in forums and communities like Reddit, Quora, and industry-specific groups to network and share your knowledge.

CREATING YOUR FREELANCE WEBSITE

Introduction

A professional website is an essential tool for freelancers. It serves as your digital business card, portfolio, and marketing platform all in one. This bonus chapter will guide you through the steps of creating a compelling and effective freelance website that attracts clients and showcases your work.

Step 1: Define Your Purpose and Goals

Before you start building your website, it's important to define its purpose and your goals. Ask yourself the following questions:

What is the primary purpose of your website?

Is it to showcase your portfolio, attract new clients, or provide information about your services?

Who is your target audience?

Understand who your potential clients are and what they are looking for.

What actions do you want visitors to take?

Do you want them to contact you, request a quote, or view your portfolio?

Having clear goals will help you design a website that meets your needs and resonates with your audience.

Step 2: Choose a Domain Name and Hosting

Domain Name:

Relevance: Choose a domain name that reflects your brand and is easy to remember. It should ideally include your name or the services you offer.

Extensions: Common extensions include .com, .net, and .org. You can also consider industry-specific extensions like .design or .consulting.

Web Hosting:

Reliability: Choose a reliable hosting provider with good uptime and customer support.

Scalability: Ensure the hosting plan can scale with your business growth.

Features: Look for features like SSL certificates for security, fast loading speeds, and easy integration with website builders.

Popular hosting providers include Bluehost, SiteGround, and HostGator.

Step 3: Select a Website Builder

There are several website builders that make it easy to create a professional-looking website without extensive technical knowledge. Some popular options include:

WordPress:

Flexibility: Highly customizable with thousands of themes and plugins.

Community: Large support community and resources.
Wix:

Ease of Use: User-friendly drag-and-drop interface.

Templates: Wide range of professional templates.

Squarespace:

Design: Sleek, modern design templates.

Integrated Features: Built-in SEO tools and e-commerce capabilities.

Choose a builder that aligns with your technical skills and the complexity of the website you want to create.

Step 4: Design Your Website

Homepage:

Headline: Craft a clear and compelling headline that immediately tells visitors what you do.

Subheadline: Provide a brief description of your services or unique selling proposition.

Call to Action (CTA): Include a strong CTA that guides visitors to the next step, such as "View My Portfolio" or "Contact Me."

About Page:

Personal Introduction: Share your background, experience, and what drives your passion for your work.

Professional Bio: Highlight your skills, achievements, and any notable projects or clients.

Photo: Include a professional photo to build a personal connection with visitors.

Services Page:

Service Descriptions: Clearly outline the services you offer. Use bullet points or sections for readability.

Benefits: Explain the benefits of your services and how they solve your clients' problems.

Pricing: If appropriate, provide pricing information or a starting price to set client expectations.

Portfolio Page:

Showcase Your Work: Display your best projects with high-quality images and detailed descriptions.

Case Studies: Include case studies that highlight the challenges, solutions, and results of your work.

Testimonials: Add client testimonials to build credibility and trust.

Contact Page:

Contact Form: Include a simple contact form for inquiries.

Email and Phone: Provide your email address and phone number for direct contact.

Social Media Links: Add links to your professional social media profiles.

Step 5: Optimize for SEO and User Experience

SEO (Search Engine Optimization):

Keywords: Research and use relevant keywords in your content to improve search engine rankings.

Meta Descriptions: Write compelling meta descriptions for each page to attract clicks from search results.

Alt Text: Add descriptive alt text to images for better search engine visibility.

User Experience (UX):

Navigation: Ensure your website has a clear and intuitive navigation menu.

Mobile-Friendly: Optimize your website for mobile devices to provide a seamless experience for all users.

Loading Speed: Use tools like Google PageSpeed Insights to check and improve your website's loading speed.

Step 6: Launch and Promote Your Website

Testing:

Review: Go through your website thoroughly to check for any errors, broken links, or missing information.

Feedback: Get feedback from friends, colleagues, or mentors to identify any areas for improvement.

Launch:

Announce: Announce the launch of your website on your social media channels, email newsletter, and any other platforms you use.

SEO: Submit your website to search engines like Google and Bing to start appearing in search results.

Promotion:

Content Marketing: Regularly update your blog with relevant content to attract visitors and improve SEO.

Social Media: Share your work, blog posts, and updates on social media to drive traffic to your website.

Networking: Include your website link in your email signature, business cards, and online profiles to increase **visibility.**

Conclusion

Creating a professional freelance website is a crucial step in establishing your online presence and attracting clients.

By defining your goals, choosing the right tools, designing an effective site, optimizing for SEO and UX, and promoting your website, you can build a powerful platform that showcases your work and grows your freelance business. Invest time and effort into your website, and it will become one of your most valuable assets in your freelancing career.

This concludes the chapter on creating your freelance website. With the right approach, your website can become a cornerstone of your professional identity, helping you connect with clients and showcase your talents to the world.

FINDING CLIENTS

Freelance Platforms

Freelance platforms are a great starting point for finding clients. They connect freelancers with clients looking for specific services. Here's how to leverage these platforms effectively:

Overview of Popular Platforms:

Upwork: One of the largest freelance marketplaces, offering projects in various fields.

Fiverr: Known for gig-based services, where freelancers offer specific tasks at set prices.

Freelancer: Similar to Upwork, with a wide range of project categories.

Toptal: Focuses on top-tier freelancers in software development, design, and finance.

Tips for Creating a Compelling Profile:

Professional Photo: Use a clear, professional headshot.

Detailed Bio: Write a concise, engaging bio that highlights your skills, experience, and what sets you apart.

Portfolio: Include your best work and ensure it is up-to-date.

Client Reviews: Encourage satisfied clients to leave positive feedback and testimonials.

Direct Outreach

Direct outreach can be a highly effective way to find clients, especially for niche or high-value projects.

Cold Emailing Techniques:

Research: Identify potential clients who could benefit from your services. Use LinkedIn, company websites, and industry directories.

Personalize Your Approach: Tailor each email to the recipient. Mention their business, explain how you can add value, and provide examples of relevant work.

Follow-Up: If you don't receive a response, follow up after a week or two. Persistence can pay off.

Networking Strategies:

Online Networking: Participate in webinars, virtual conferences, and online meetups. Engage in discussions and connect with attendees.

Offline Networking: Attend industry conferences, local meetups, and networking events. Bring business cards and follow up with new contacts.

Local to Global

Starting with local clients can help you build a strong foundation before expanding globally.

Leveraging Local Clients for International Exposure:

Build a Strong Local Reputation: Deliver high-quality work and build strong relationships with local clients.

Ask for Referrals: Encourage satisfied local clients to refer you to their international contacts.

Attending Conferences and Meetups:

Industry Events: Attend events that attract international participants. These can be excellent opportunities to meet potential clients face-to-face.

Speaking Engagements: If possible, participate as a speaker or panelist. This positions you as an expert and increases your visibility.

By preparing thoroughly and utilizing various strategies to find clients, you can position yourself for success as a global freelancer. The next chapters will delve deeper into marketing yourself, managing international projects, and building long-term client relationships.

MARKETING YOURSELF

Branding for Freelancers

Creating a personal brand is essential for standing out in the competitive world of freelancing. Your brand is the perception that clients have of you and your work. Here's how to develop a strong personal brand:

Creating a Personal Brand:

Identify Your Unique Selling Proposition (USP): Determine what sets you apart from other freelancers. This could be a specific skill, a unique approach, or an industry specialization.

Define Your Brand Voice: Your brand voice should reflect your personality and values. Are you professional and formal, or casual and friendly? Consistency is key.

Consistent Messaging:

Visual Identity: Develop a consistent visual identity that includes a logo, color scheme, and typography. Use these elements across all your marketing materials.

Brand Story: Craft a compelling brand story that explains who you are, what you do, and why you do it. Share this on your website and social media profiles.

Content Marketing

Content marketing is a powerful way to showcase your expertise and attract potential clients. By creating valuable content, you can establish yourself as an authority in your field.

Blogging and Vlogging:

Blogging: Write informative blog posts on topics relevant to your industry. Use SEO techniques to increase visibility and attract organic traffic.

Vlogging: Create video content to engage your audience. Tutorials, behind-the-scenes videos, and client testimonials can be highly effective.

Webinars and Online Courses:

Webinars: Host webinars to share your knowledge and interact with potential clients. Promote your webinars through email marketing and social media.

Online Courses: Develop online courses to teach others your skills. Platforms like Teachable and Udemy make it easy to create and sell courses.

Social Media Strategies

Social media platforms are essential for building your brand and reaching potential clients. Here's how to use them effectively:

Choosing the Right Platforms:

LinkedIn: Ideal for professional networking and B2B marketing. Share industry insights, engage in discussions, and connect with potential clients.

Twitter: Great for sharing quick updates, industry news, and engaging with a broader audience.

Instagram: Best for visual content. Showcase your work, share behind-the-scenes looks, and use hashtags to increase reach.

Engaging with Your Audience:

Regular Updates: Post consistently to keep your audience engaged. Use a content calendar to plan your posts.

Interaction: Respond to comments, join discussions, and engage with other users' content. Building relationships on social media can lead to client opportunities.

MARKETING YOUR BUSINESS AND WINNING CLIENTS

Introduction

Marketing your freelance business effectively is crucial for attracting and winning clients. A strategic approach to marketing helps you stand out in a crowded market, showcase your expertise, and build a strong client base.

This chapter provides comprehensive strategies for marketing your freelance business and tips on how to win clients.

Step 1: Build a Strong Online Presence

Professional Website:

Design and Usability: Ensure your website is professional, user-friendly, and mobile-responsive. It should clearly communicate your services, showcase your portfolio, and include a call-to-action.

SEO Optimization: Optimize your website for search engines by using relevant keywords, meta descriptions, and high-quality content. This helps potential clients find you more easily.

Social Media Profiles:

Platform Selection: Choose the social media platforms that are most relevant to your industry and target audience (e.g., LinkedIn, Twitter, Instagram).

Consistent Branding: Ensure your branding is consistent across all social media profiles. Use the same profile picture, handle, and bio information.

Content Marketing:

Blogging: Start a blog on your website where you share valuable insights, tips, and industry trends. This positions you as an expert in your field and improves your SEO.

Guest Posting: Write guest posts for reputable websites in your industry. This helps you reach a wider audience and build credibility.

Step 2: Networking and Building Relationships

Professional Associations:

Join Associations: Become a member of professional associations related to your industry. These organizations provide networking opportunities, resources, and industry insights.

Attend Events: Participate in industry conferences, webinars, and workshops. These events are excellent for networking and staying updated on industry trends.

Online Communities:

Forums and Groups: Join online forums, LinkedIn groups, and Facebook groups related to your field. Engage in discussions, offer advice, and connect with other professionals.

Networking Platforms: Use platforms like LinkedIn to connect with potential clients, peers, and industry leaders. Regularly engage with your network by sharing content and commenting on posts.

Local Networking:

Meetups: Attend local networking events and meetups. These gatherings can help you build relationships with potential clients and local businesses.

Chambers of Commerce: Join your local chamber of commerce to connect with other business owners and participate in community events.

Step 3: Utilize Freelance Platforms

Profile Optimization:

Complete Profile: Ensure your profile is complete with a professional photo, detailed bio, and comprehensive list of services.

Portfolio: Showcase your best work in your portfolio. Include case studies, client testimonials, and project details.

Bidding on Projects:

Targeted Bidding: Focus on projects that match your skills and experience. Tailor your proposals to address the specific needs of each project.

Competitive Pricing: Research market rates and price your services competitively. Offer value by highlighting your unique skills and past successes.

Client Reviews:

Request Reviews: Ask satisfied clients to leave positive reviews on your profile. High ratings and positive feedback can significantly increase your chances of winning new clients.

Respond to Feedback: Engage with client reviews by thanking them for positive feedback and addressing any concerns raised in negative reviews.

Step 4: Create Compelling Proposals

Understand Client Needs:

Research: Thoroughly research the client's business, industry, and specific project requirements. This shows your dedication and helps tailor your proposal.

Ask Questions: Clarify any uncertainties by asking the client detailed questions about their needs and expectations.

Tailored Solutions:

Personalized Proposals: Customize each proposal to address the specific needs and goals of the client. Highlight how your skills and experience align with their project.

Value Proposition: Clearly articulate the value you bring to the project. Focus on the benefits and outcomes the cli
ent will receive from your services.

Professional Presentation:

Structure and Format: Use a clear and professional format for your proposals. Include sections like introduction, project understanding, proposed solution, timeline, pricing, and next steps.

Visuals: Enhance your proposals with visuals such as charts, graphs, and images. This makes your proposal more engaging and easier to understand.

Step 5: Leverage Testimonials and Case Studies

Collect Testimonials:

Client Requests: After completing a project, ask your clients for testimonials. Provide guidance on key points they could mention to highlight your strengths.

Display Testimonials: Feature client testimonials prominently on your website, social media profiles, and marketing materials.

Develop Case Studies:

Project Details: Create detailed case studies that outline the challenges, solutions, and results of your projects. Include metrics and measurable outcomes.

Visual Appeal: Design your case studies to be visually appealing and easy to read. Use headings, bullet points, and images to break up text.

Step 6: Offer Free Value

Free Resources:

E-books and Guides: Create valuable e-books or guides related to your services. Offer these as free downloads on your website to attract potential clients.

Templates and Tools: Develop templates, checklists, or tools that your target audience can use. These resources showcase your expertise and provide value.

Webinars and Workshops:

Educational Content: Host webinars or workshops on topics relevant to your industry. This positions you as an expert and provides an opportunity to engage with potential clients.

Follow-Up: After the event, follow up with attendees to thank them for participating and offer additional resources or consultations.

Step 7: Develop a Referral Program

Incentivize Referrals:

Referral Rewards: Offer incentives such as discounts, free services, or gift cards to clients who refer new business to you.

Clear Guidelines: Provide clear guidelines on how your referral program works and the rewards clients can expect.

Promote Your Program:

Communication: Regularly communicate your referral program to existing clients through newsletters, social media, and direct emails.

Reminders: Periodically remind clients about the referral program, especially after completing successful projects.

Step 8: Continuous Improvement and Learning

Feedback and Adaptation:

Client Feedback: Regularly seek feedback from clients to understand their satisfaction and areas for improvement. Use this feedback to refine your services and processes.

Market Trends: Stay updated on industry trends and changes in client preferences. Adapt your services and marketing strategies accordingly.

Professional Development:

Courses and Certifications: Invest in courses and certifications to enhance your skills and knowledge. This not only improves your service quality but also adds credibility.

Networking and Mentorship: Join professional networks and seek mentorship from experienced freelancers. Learning from others can provide valuable insights and guidance.

Conclusion

Marketing your freelance business effectively requires a strategic approach that includes building a strong online presence, networking, utilizing freelance platforms, creating compelling proposals, leveraging testimonials, offering free value, developing a referral program, and continuously improving your skills and services.

By implementing these strategies, you can attract and win clients, build a solid reputation, and ensure the long-term success of your freelance business.

This chapter on marketing your business and how to win clients provides actionable strategies and tips to help you effectively promote your freelance services and secure more clients. By focusing on these areas, you can enhance your visibility, demonstrate your value, and grow your freelance career. Happy marketing!

MANAGING INTERNATIONAL PROJECTS

Time Zone Management

Working with international clients means dealing with different time zones. Effective time zone management ensures smooth communication and project delivery.

Tools and Techniques for Managing Different Time Zones:

Time Zone Converters: Use tools like World Time Buddy or Time Zone Converter to keep track of different time zones.

Shared Calendars: Google Calendar and other shared calendars can help coordinate meeting times with clients.

Setting Expectations with Clients:

Clear Communication: Clearly communicate your working hours and availability. Include this information in your initial client discussions and project proposals.

Regular Updates: Provide regular project updates and check-ins to keep clients informed, regardless of time differences.

Cross-Cultural Communication

Effective communication is crucial when working with clients from different cultures. Understanding cultural nuances can improve your client relationships and project outcomes.

Understanding Cultural Nuances:

Research: Learn about your clients' cultural backgrounds. Understanding their communication styles, business etiquette, and decision-making processes can help you interact more effectively.

Respect and Adaptation: Show respect for cultural differences and be willing to adapt your approach as needed.

Effective Communication Strategies:

Clear and Concise Communication: Use clear and concise language to avoid misunderstandings. Avoid jargon and idiomatic expressions that may not be understood.

Active Listening: Practice active listening to ensure you understand your clients' needs and concerns. Confirm your understanding by summarizing key points.

Project Management Tools

Using the right project management tools can streamline your workflow and ensure successful project completion.

Overview of Popular Tools:

Trello: A visual project management tool that uses boards and cards to organize tasks. Ideal for tracking progress and collaborating with clients.

Asana: A comprehensive project management tool that offers task lists, timelines, and team collaboration features.

Slack: A communication tool that facilitates real-time messaging and file sharing. Integrates with other project management tools for seamless collaboration.

Best Practices for Remote Project Management:

Set Clear Goals and Milestones: Define project goals, deliverables, and milestones at the outset. Use project management tools to track progress and deadlines.

Regular Check-Ins: Schedule regular check-ins with clients to review progress, address any issues, and adjust plans as needed.

Documentation: Maintain thorough documentation of project details, communication, and decisions. This helps ensure clarity and accountability.

By implementing these strategies, you can effectively market yourself, manage international projects, and build strong relationships with clients worldwide. The next chapters will explore legal and financial considerations, building long-term client relationships, and scaling your freelance business.

LEGAL AND FINANCIAL CONSIDERATIONS

Contracts and Agreements

One of the most crucial aspects of freelancing, especially on a global scale, is ensuring that you have solid contracts and agreements in place. These documents protect both you and your clients by clearly defining the terms of your working relationship.

Essential Clauses for International Contracts:

Scope of Work: Clearly outline the tasks, deliverables, and deadlines. Specify what is included and what is not included in the project.

Payment Terms: Define the payment structure, including rates, due dates, and preferred payment methods. Include details about deposits, milestones, and final payments.

Intellectual Property Rights: Specify who owns the intellectual property (IP) created during the project. Typically, freelancers retain ownership until final payment is received.

Confidentiality and Non-Disclosure: Include clauses to protect sensitive information exchanged during the project.

Termination Clause: Outline the conditions under which the contract can be terminated by either party and the consequences of such termination.

Protecting Your Intellectual Property:

Copyright: Ensure your contracts specify that you retain the copyright to your work until payment is received.

Trademark: If you develop any trademarks for a client, specify the transfer of trademark rights in the contract.

Non-Compete Clauses: Include clauses that prevent the client from using your work to compete directly with you.

Taxation and Invoicing

Handling international taxation and invoicing can be complex, but it's essential for maintaining a professional and compliant freelance business.

Understanding International Tax Obligations:

Tax Residency: Determine where you are considered a tax resident and understand the tax obligations in that country.

Double Taxation Treaties: Research if there are treaties between your country and your client's country to avoid being taxed twice on the same income.

VAT and GST: Understand the rules for Value Added Tax (VAT) or Goods and Services Tax (GST) when working with international clients.

Tools for Invoicing and Payment Processing:

Invoicing Software: Use tools like FreshBooks, QuickBooks, or Xero to create and manage invoices. These tools often integrate with payment processors and accounting software.

Payment Processors: Platforms like PayPal, Stripe, and TransferWise facilitate international payments and can handle currency conversions.

Invoice Details: Ensure your invoices include all necessary details: your contact information, client information, project description, payment terms, and due dates.

Insurance and Liability

Freelancers must consider various types of insurance to protect their business and manage liability risks.

Freelance Insurance Options:

Professional Liability Insurance: Also known as Errors and Omissions (E&O) insurance, this protects you against claims of negligence or inadequate work.

General Liability Insurance: Covers claims of bodily injury or property damage caused by your business activities.

Health and Disability Insurance: Ensure you have adequate health and disability coverage, especially if you are working without the safety net of an employer.

Managing Liability Risks:

Client Vetting: Screen potential clients to ensure they are reputable and financially stable.

Clear Communication: Maintain open and clear communication with clients to manage expectations and avoid misunderstandings.

Record Keeping: Keep detailed records of all communications, contracts, and work completed. This documentation can be vital if a dispute arises.

Case Studies: Navigating Legal and Financial Challenges

Learning from the experiences of other freelancers can provide valuable insights into managing legal and financial challenges.

Case Study 1: Protecting Intellectual Property:

Scenario: A freelance graphic designer created a logo for a client who later used it without completing the final payment.

Solution: The designer had a clear contract specifying IP rights and was able to take legal action to secure payment and IP protection.

Case Study 2: Handling International Taxation:

Scenario: A freelance consultant working with clients in multiple countries faced issues with double taxation.

Solution: By consulting a tax advisor, the consultant leveraged double taxation treaties and optimized their tax strategy to minimize liabilities.

Case Study 3: Insurance and Liability:

Scenario: A freelance web developer faced a lawsuit from a client claiming a website malfunction caused significant business losses.

Solution: The developer's professional liability insurance covered legal fees and settlement costs, preventing a financial disaster.

Navigating the legal and financial aspects of global freelancing requires diligence and proactive planning. By ensuring you have robust contracts, understanding your tax obligations, and securing appropriate insurance, you can protect your business and focus on delivering exceptional work to your clients.

The next chapters will guide you through building long-term client relationships and scaling your freelance business for sustained success.

BUILDING LONG-TERM CLIENT RELATIONSHIPS

Customer Service Excellence

Providing exceptional customer service is the foundation for building long-term client relationships. Clients remember how you made them feel just as much as the work you delivered. Here's how to ensure you're offering top-notch customer service:

Understanding Client Needs:

Initial Consultations: Spend time understanding your clients' goals, expectations, and challenges. Ask open-ended questions to gather comprehensive insights.

Tailored Solutions: Offer solutions that are specifically tailored to meet your clients' unique needs. Show them that you understand their business and are invested in their success.

Effective Communication:

Regular Updates: Keep your clients informed with regular updates on the progress of their projects. Use their preferred communication channels and be responsive to their queries.

Transparency: Be transparent about timelines, potential challenges, and any changes that may arise. Honesty builds trust and credibility.

Problem Resolution:

Proactive Approach: Anticipate potential issues and address them before they become problems. Offer solutions and alternatives to keep projects on track.

Apologize and Rectify: If something goes wrong, apologize sincerely and take immediate steps to rectify the situation. Clients appreciate a freelancer who owns their mistakes and fixes them promptly.

Retaining Clients

Retaining clients is more cost-effective than acquiring new ones and leads to a stable, predictable income. Here are strategies to ensure clients keep coming back:

Consistent Quality:

Deliver Excellence: Always strive to deliver high-quality work that meets or exceeds client expectations. Consistency builds trust and reliability.

Continuous Improvement: Seek feedback from clients and use it to improve your services. Show clients that you are committed to growing and evolving with their needs.

Building Relationships:

Personal Connection: Build personal connections with your clients. Remember details about their business, their preferences, and their milestones.

Regular Check-Ins: Even when you're not working on a project, check in with your clients periodically. Ask how they are doing and if there are any upcoming needs you can help with.

Adding Value:

Free Extras: Occasionally offer small, free extras to add value to your services. This could be a quick consultation, an additional feature, or helpful resources.

Educational Content: Share industry insights, tips, and updates that could benefit your clients. This positions you as a valuable resource and keeps you top-of-mind.

Upselling and Cross-Selling Services

Expanding the scope of your services with existing clients can increase your revenue and deepen your relationship with them. Here's how to approach upselling and cross-selling:

Identify Opportunities:

Client Needs Assessment: Regularly assess your clients' evolving needs. Look for gaps in their operations or areas where additional services could add value.

Proactive Suggestions: Suggest additional services that can help your clients achieve their goals. Be specific about how these services will benefit them.

Package Deals:

Bundling Services: Create service packages that combine complementary services at a discounted rate. This makes it easier for clients to see the value in purchasing multiple services.

Retainer Agreements: Offer retainer agreements for ongoing services. This provides a steady income stream for you and ensures clients receive continuous support.

Demonstrating Value:

Case Studies and Success Stories: Use case studies and success stories to demonstrate the value of your additional services. Show how other clients have benefited from the same offerings.

Metrics and ROI: Provide metrics and projected return on investment (ROI) to justify the cost of additional services. Clients are more likely to invest when they see clear, quantifiable benefits.

Testimonials and Referrals

Positive testimonials and referrals are powerful tools for building credibility and attracting new clients. Here's how to leverage them effectively:

Gathering Testimonials:

Requesting Feedback: After completing a project, ask your clients for feedback. Encourage them to share their positive experiences in a testimonial.

Highlighting Results: Guide clients to mention specific results and benefits they experienced from your work. Detailed testimonials are more persuasive.

Showcasing Testimonials:

Website: Display testimonials prominently on your website. Use a dedicated testimonials page and highlight them on your homepage and service pages.

Social Media and Profiles: Share testimonials on your social media profiles and freelance platform profiles. This increases your credibility and visibility.

Encouraging Referrals:

Referral Incentives: Offer incentives for clients who refer new business to you. This could be a discount on future services, a gift card, or a free consultation.

Easy Referral Process: Make it easy for clients to refer others to you. Provide them with a referral template or a unique referral link to share.

Case Studies: Building Long-Term Client Relationships
Learning from real-world examples can provide practical insights into building and maintaining long-term client relationships.

Case Study 1: Exceeding Expectations:

Scenario: A freelance web developer consistently delivered high-quality projects on time, anticipating client needs and offering innovative solutions.

Outcome: The client was so impressed that they referred several other businesses, leading to a steady stream of new projects.

Case Study 2: Effective Upselling:

Scenario: A freelance marketer identified that a client could benefit from additional SEO services. After presenting a detailed proposal and projected ROI, the client agreed to the expanded services.

Outcome: The client saw significant improvements in their search rankings and traffic, and the freelancer secured a long-term contract with ongoing work.

Case Study 3: Leveraging Testimonials:

Scenario: A graphic designer collected detailed testimonials from satisfied clients and showcased them on their website and social media profiles.

Outcome: The testimonials built credibility and attracted high-profile clients, leading to increased business and higher rates.

Building long-term client relationships is crucial for sustained success as a freelancer. By providing exceptional customer service, retaining clients, upselling and cross-selling services, and leveraging testimonials and referrals, you can create a loyal client base and a stable income stream.

The next chapters will guide you through scaling your freelance business and preparing for the future of global freelancing.

THE BEST COUNTRIES TO FREELANCE FROM

Introduction

One of the great advantages of freelancing is the flexibility to work from virtually anywhere in the world.

However, some countries offer better conditions for freelancers in terms of cost of living, internet connectivity, quality of life, and community. This chapter explores some of the best countries for freelancers, highlighting their unique advantages and considerations.

Key Factors to Consider

When choosing a country to freelance from, consider the following factors:

Cost of Living:

Affordable housing, food, transportation, and healthcare can make a big difference in your overall quality of life and financial stability.

Internet Connectivity:

Reliable and fast internet is essential for remote work, video calls, and accessing online platforms.

Quality of Life:

Consider factors such as safety, healthcare, education, and recreational activities.

Community and Networking:

Being part of a vibrant freelancer or digital nomad community can provide support, networking opportunities, and social interaction.

Visa and Tax Regulations:

Understanding the visa requirements and tax implications for freelancers is crucial for long-term planning.

Top Countries for Freelancers

Portugal:

Cost of Living: Moderate. Cities like Lisbon and Porto offer a good balance of affordability and amenities.

Internet Connectivity: Excellent, with widespread availability of high-speed internet.

Quality of Life: High. Portugal offers a mild climate, beautiful landscapes, and a relaxed lifestyle.

Community: Lisbon has a thriving digital nomad community with co-working spaces and regular meetups.

Visa and Taxes: The D7 visa is designed for remote workers and freelancers. Portugal also offers favorable tax conditions for new residents.

Thailand:

Cost of Living: Low. Cities like Chiang Mai and Bangkok are popular for their affordability.

Internet Connectivity: Good, especially in urban areas and co-working spaces.

Quality of Life: High. Thailand offers rich culture, excellent food, and a warm climate.

Community: Chiang Mai is a well-known hub for digital nomads, with a large, active community.

Visa and Taxes: The Smart Visa program includes options for freelancers and digital nomads.

Estonia:

Cost of Living: Moderate. Tallinn offers a balance of affordability and European city amenities.

Internet Connectivity: Excellent, with extensive Wi-Fi availability.

Quality of Life: High. Estonia is known for its digital infrastructure, safety, and clean environment.

Community: Growing digital nomad and startup communities, especially in Tallinn.

Visa and Taxes: The e-Residency program allows freelancers to establish and run a location-independent business.

Mexico:

Cost of Living: Low to moderate. Cities like Mexico City and Playa del Carmen offer different levels of affordability.

Internet Connectivity: Good, particularly in urban areas and digital nomad hotspots.

Quality of Life: High. Mexico offers diverse landscapes, rich culture, and warm weather.

Community: Playa del Carmen and Mexico City have vibrant digital nomad communities.

Visa and Taxes: The Temporary Resident Visa is suitable for freelancers staying longer than six months.

Georgia:

Cost of Living: Low. Tbilisi offers great value for money.
Internet Connectivity: Good, with reliable internet in urban areas.

Quality of Life: High. Georgia offers a low cost of living, scenic beauty, and a rich cultural history.

Community: Tbilisi is becoming increasingly popular with digital nomads.

Visa and Taxes: Citizens of many countries can stay visa-free for up to one year. Georgia offers favorable tax conditions for foreign entrepreneurs.

Spain:

Cost of Living: Moderate to high. Cities like Barcelona and Madrid are more expensive, while smaller towns offer more affordability.

Internet Connectivity: Excellent, with widespread high-speed internet.

Quality of Life: High. Spain offers a great lifestyle with good healthcare, education, and vibrant culture.

Community: Barcelona and Madrid have large expat and digital nomad communities.

Visa and Taxes: The Non-Lucrative Visa allows freelancers to live in Spain, though tax regulations can be complex.

Vietnam:

Cost of Living: Low. Cities like Ho Chi Minh City and Hanoi are very affordable.

Internet Connectivity: Good, especially in urban areas.
Quality of Life: High. Vietnam offers a rich cultural experience, delicious cuisine, and beautiful landscapes.

Community: Ho Chi Minh City and Hanoi have growing digital nomad communities.

Visa and Taxes: The e-Visa allows stays of up to 30 days, with options for longer stays through business visas.

Indonesia (Bali):

Cost of Living: Low to moderate. Bali offers various levels of affordability depending on the area.

Internet Connectivity: Good in co-working spaces and urban areas.

Quality of Life: High. Bali offers a unique blend of natural beauty, culture, and a relaxed lifestyle.

Community: Bali has a large and active digital nomad community.

Visa and Taxes: The Visa on Arrival allows stays of up to 30 days, with options to extend.

Tips for Choosing the Right Country

Research: Thoroughly research the countries you are interested in. Look into the cost of living, internet speed, quality of life, and local communities.

Visit First: If possible, visit the country before making a long-term commitment. This can give you a better sense of whether it's a good fit for your lifestyle and work needs.

Join Forums and Groups: Join online forums and social media groups related to digital nomads and freelancers in the countries you are considering. These can provide valuable insights and firsthand experiences.

Plan for Visas and Taxes: Understand the visa requirements and tax implications of living in a particular country as a freelancer. Consulting with a legal or tax professional can help you navigate these aspects.

Consider Time Zones: If you have clients in specific regions, consider the time zone differences and how they will affect your work schedule.

Conclusion

Choosing the right country to freelance from can enhance your work-life balance, productivity, and overall well-being. By considering factors such as cost of living, internet connectivity, quality of life, and community, you can find a location that suits your professional and personal needs.

Whether you prefer the vibrant culture of Thailand, the digital infrastructure of Estonia, or the scenic beauty of Portugal, there are numerous options available for freelancers looking to work globally.

This chapter on the best countries to freelance from provides an overview of top destinations that offer favorable conditions for freelancers. By selecting the right location, you can enjoy a fulfilling and successful freelance career while exploring the world. Happy travels and happy freelancing!

TWENTY IDEAS FOR FREELANCE BUSINESSES

Introduction

Freelancing offers a world of possibilities for those with diverse skills and interests. Whether you're starting your freelance journey or looking to expand your business, exploring different freelance business ideas can spark inspiration and help you find your niche. This chapter presents twenty ideas for freelance businesses, covering a range of industries and services.

1. Content Writing and Copywriting

Overview:

Create engaging and persuasive content for websites, blogs, marketing materials, and more.

Specialize in areas like SEO writing, technical writing, or creative writing.

Skills Needed:

Strong writing and grammar skills.
Ability to research and understand various topics.

Getting Started:

Build a portfolio with diverse writing samples.
Use platforms like Upwork, Freelancer, and ProBlogger to find clients.

2. Graphic Design

Overview:

Design visual content such as logos, brochures, social media graphics, and websites.
Specialize in branding, illustration, or web design.

Skills Needed:

Proficiency in design software (e.g., Adobe Creative Suite).
Strong creative and artistic skills.

Getting Started:

Create a portfolio showcasing your best work.
Join design communities and platforms like Behance and Dribbble.

3. Web Development

Overview:

Build and maintain websites for businesses, individuals, and organizations.
Specialize in front-end, back-end, or full-stack development.

Skills Needed:

Proficiency in coding languages (e.g., HTML, CSS, JavaScript, Python).
Understanding of web design principles and user experience.

Getting Started:

Develop a portfolio of websites you've built.
Use platforms like GitHub to showcase your code and projects.

4. Digital Marketing

Overview:

Help businesses grow their online presence through SEO, social media marketing, email marketing, and more.
Specialize in specific areas like content marketing, PPC advertising, or influencer marketing.

Skills Needed:

Knowledge of digital marketing strategies and tools.
Analytical skills to measure and optimize campaigns.

Getting Started:

Obtain certifications (e.g., Google Analytics, HubSpot).
Build a portfolio of successful marketing campaigns.

5. Virtual Assistance

Overview:

Provide administrative support to businesses and entrepreneurs remotely.
Specialize in tasks like email management, scheduling, data entry, and customer support.

Skills Needed:

Strong organizational and communication skills.
Proficiency in office software (e.g., Microsoft Office, Google Workspace).

Getting Started:

Highlight your administrative skills and experience in your profile.
Use platforms like Virtual Assistant Jobs and Belay to find clients.

6. Social Media Management

Overview:

Manage and grow social media accounts for businesses and individuals.
Create content, engage with followers, and analyze social media performance.

Skills Needed:

Knowledge of various social media platforms and their best practices.
Creative content creation and communication skills.

Getting Started:

Build a portfolio of social media accounts you've managed.
Offer your services on platforms like Hootsuite, Buffer, and SocialBee.

7. Photography

Overview:

Provide photography services for events, portraits, products, and more.
Specialize in niches like wedding photography, commercial photography, or travel photography.

Skills Needed:

Proficiency with camera equipment and editing software.
Strong creative and technical photography skills.

Getting Started:

Create a portfolio showcasing your photography work.
Use platforms like Shutterstock, Adobe Stock, and Fiverr to sell your photos and services.

8. Video Production and Editing

Overview:

Create and edit video content for businesses, events, and online platforms.
Specialize in areas like promotional videos, documentaries, or YouTube content.

Skills Needed:

Proficiency in video editing software (e.g., Adobe Premiere Pro, Final Cut Pro).
Strong storytelling and creative skills.

Getting Started:

Build a portfolio of video projects you've completed.
Use platforms like Upwork, Fiverr, and Vimeo to showcase your work.

9. Coaching and Consulting

Overview:

Provide expert advice and guidance in areas like business, career development, health, or personal growth.
Specialize in niches like executive coaching, life coaching, or wellness consulting.

Skills Needed:

Expertise in your chosen field.
Strong communication and interpersonal skills.

Getting Started:

Obtain relevant certifications and build a client base through networking.
Use platforms like Coach.me, Clarity.fm, and LinkedIn to offer your services.

10. Translation and Interpretation

Overview:

Translate written content or provide interpretation services for businesses and individuals.
Specialize in specific languages or industries (e.g., legal, medical, technical).

Skills Needed:

Proficiency in multiple languages.

Strong writing and communication skills.

Getting Started:

Create a portfolio of translation work.
Use platforms like ProZ, TranslatorsCafe, and Upwork to find clients.

11. UX/UI Design

Overview:

Design user experiences and interfaces for websites, apps, and software.
Specialize in user research, wireframing, prototyping, and usability testing.

Skills Needed:

Proficiency in design tools (e.g., Sketch, Figma, Adobe XD).
Strong understanding of user-centered design principles.

Getting Started:

Build a portfolio showcasing your UX/UI design projects.
Join design communities and use platforms like Dribbble and Behance.

12. Accounting and Bookkeeping

Overview:

Provide financial management services, including bookkeeping, tax preparation, and financial planning. Specialize in specific industries or types of businesses.

Skills Needed:

Knowledge of accounting principles and software (e.g., QuickBooks, Xero).
Strong attention to detail and analytical skills.

Getting Started:

Obtain relevant certifications (e.g., CPA, QuickBooks ProAdvisor).
Offer your services on platforms like Upwork, Freelancer, and LinkedIn.

13. Public Relations

Overview:

Help businesses manage their public image and media relations.
Specialize in media outreach, press release writing, and crisis management.

Skills Needed:

Strong communication and writing skills.
Knowledge of media relations and PR strategies.

Getting Started:

Build a portfolio of successful PR campaigns.
Use platforms like Cision, PR Newswire, and Muck Rack to find clients.

14. Voiceover Acting

Overview:

Provide voiceover services for commercials, animations, audiobooks, and more.
Specialize in specific niches like character voices, narration, or corporate videos.

Skills Needed:

Strong vocal skills and the ability to interpret scripts.
Access to recording equipment and editing software.

Getting Started:

Create a demo reel showcasing your voiceover work.
Use platforms like Voices.com, Voice123, and Fiverr to find clients.

15. E-commerce Management

Overview:

Manage online stores for businesses, handling tasks like product listings, customer service, and marketing.

Specialize in platforms like Shopify, Amazon, or Etsy.

Skills Needed:

Knowledge of e-commerce platforms and digital marketing.
Strong organizational and customer service skills.

Getting Started:

Build a portfolio of e-commerce projects you've managed.
Offer your services on platforms like Upwork, Freelancer, and LinkedIn.

16. App Development

Overview:

Develop mobile applications for iOS and Android devices.
Specialize in specific types of apps, such as games, productivity tools, or social media.

Skills Needed:

Proficiency in coding languages (e.g., Swift, Kotlin, Java).
Strong problem-solving and technical skills.

Getting Started:

Develop a portfolio of apps you've created.
Use platforms like GitHub to showcase your code and projects.

17. Event Planning

Overview:

Plan and coordinate events such as weddings, corporate events, and parties.
Specialize in specific types of events or industries.

Skills Needed:

Strong organizational and project management skills.
Excellent communication and negotiation abilities.

Getting Started:

Build a portfolio of events you've planned.
Join professional organizations like the Meeting Professionals International (MPI) and use platforms like Eventbrite and LinkedIn.

18. Podcast Production

Overview:

Produce, edit, and distribute podcasts for businesses or individuals.
Specialize in content creation, audio editing, and marketing.

Skills Needed:

Proficiency in audio editing software (e.g., Audacity, Adobe Audition).
Strong storytelling and content creation skills.

Getting Started:

Create a portfolio of podcasts you've produced.
Use platforms like Podbean, Anchor, and Fiverr to find clients.

19. Health and Wellness Coaching

Overview:

Provide guidance and support for individuals looking to improve their health and wellness.
Specialize in areas like nutrition, fitness, mental health, or holistic wellness.

Skills Needed:

Relevant certifications (e.g., personal training, nutrition coaching).
Strong communication and motivational skills.

Getting Started:

Build a portfolio of success stories and client testimonials.
Offer your services on platforms like Coach.me, Thumbtack, and LinkedIn.

20. Legal Consulting

Overview:

Provide legal advice and services to businesses and individuals.
Specialize in areas like corporate law, intellectual property, or family law.

Skills Needed:

Relevant legal qualifications and experience.
Strong analytical and communication skills.

Getting Started:

Build a portfolio of your legal expertise and case studies.
Offer your services on platforms like UpCounsel, Clarity.fm, and LinkedIn.

Conclusion

Freelancing offers endless opportunities for those willing to leverage their skills and passions. Whether you're a creative professional, a technical expert, or a business strategist, there's a freelance business idea that can align with your talents and interests. Explore these ideas, find your niche, and embark on a fulfilling and flexible career as a freelancer.

This chapter on twenty ideas for freelance businesses provides a starting point for exploring various opportunities in the freelance world. By identifying your strengths and interests, you can choose a path that offers both professional satisfaction and financial success.

HOW TO CHARGE FOR YOUR TIME AS A FREELANCER

Introduction

Setting the right rates for your freelance services is crucial for your business's success and sustainability. Charging appropriately for your time ensures that you are compensated fairly for your skills and effort, while also aligning with market expectations.

This chapter will guide you through the process of determining how to charge for your time as a freelancer, covering various pricing models, factors to consider, and tips for communicating your rates to clients.

Step 1: Understand Different Pricing Models

Hourly Rate:

Charge clients based on the number of hours you work. This model is straightforward and transparent, making it easy to track and bill for your time.

Advantages: Flexible, easy to calculate.

Disadvantages: Potentially limited earning potential if not managed efficiently.

Fixed Project Rate:

Charge a flat fee for the entire project, regardless of the time it takes to complete. This model works well for clearly defined projects with specific deliverables.

Advantages: Predictable income, aligns with value delivered.

Disadvantages: Risk of underestimating the time required.

Retainer:

Charge a recurring fee for a set amount of work over a specified period (e.g., monthly). This model provides steady income and long-term client relationships.

Advantages: Stable income, ongoing work.

Disadvantages: Requires consistent workload management.

Value-Based Pricing:

Charge based on the value your work delivers to the client, rather than the time or effort involved. This model aligns your earnings with the impact of your work.

Advantages: Potential for higher earnings, focuses on value.

Disadvantages: More challenging to justify and communicate.

Step 2: Calculate Your Base Rate

Determine Your Expenses:

List all your business and personal expenses, including rent, utilities, insurance, software subscriptions, taxes, and any other costs.

Set Your Income Goals:

Decide how much you want to earn annually, taking into account your living expenses, savings goals, and desired lifestyle.

Estimate Billable Hours:

Calculate the number of hours you can realistically bill clients each year. Consider time spent on non-billable activities like marketing, administration, and professional development.

Calculate Your Hourly Rate:

Use the following formula to determine your base hourly rate:

Hourly Rate
=
Annual Income Goal
+
Annual Expenses

Billable Hours

Hourly Rate=
Billable Hours

Annual Income Goal+Annual Expenses

Step 3: Research Market Rates

Industry Standards:

Research average rates in your industry and for your specific services. Use resources like industry surveys, freelance platforms, and professional associations to gather data.

Competitor Analysis:

Look at what other freelancers with similar skills and experience are charging. Consider the range of rates and where you fit within that spectrum.

Location-Based Rates:

Take into account the geographic location of your clients. Rates can vary significantly based on the cost of living and market conditions in different regions.

Step 4: Adjust for Experience and Expertise

Experience Level:

Adjust your rates based on your years of experience and the depth of your expertise. More experienced freelancers can typically charge higher rates.

Specialized Skills:

If you have specialized skills or certifications that are in high demand, you can justify higher rates.

Portfolio and Reputation:

A strong portfolio and positive client testimonials can support higher rates. Demonstrate the quality and impact of your work to potential clients.

Step 5: Communicate Your Rates to Clients

Transparency:

Be clear and upfront about your rates and pricing structure. Provide detailed information on what is included in your rates and any additional costs that may apply.

Professionalism:

Present your rates professionally, whether through a formal proposal, a rate card, or a detailed email. Ensure that your communication is clear, concise, and well-organized.

Value Proposition:

Emphasize the value you bring to the client. Highlight your skills, experience, and the benefits of your services. Use case studies and testimonials to demonstrate your impact.

Negotiation:

Be prepared to negotiate with clients. Understand your minimum acceptable rate and be willing to walk away if the client cannot meet your terms.

Step 6: Review and Adjust Regularly

Annual Review:

Review your rates annually to ensure they reflect your growing experience, increased costs, and market changes.

Client Feedback:

Gather feedback from clients to understand their perception of your value and adjust your rates accordingly.

Economic Conditions:

Stay informed about economic trends and industry shifts that may impact your rates. Adjust your pricing strategy to remain competitive and profitable.

Conclusion

Determining how to charge for your time as a freelancer involves understanding different pricing models, calculating your base rate, researching market rates, adjusting for experience and expertise, and effectively communicating your rates to clients.

By following these steps, you can set fair and competitive rates that reflect your value and support your business's success. Regularly reviewing and adjusting your rates ensures that you remain aligned with market conditions and your evolving skills.

This chapter on how to charge for your time as a freelancer provides a comprehensive guide to setting and communicating your rates. By establishing a solid pricing strategy, you can ensure that you are fairly compensated for your work and build a sustainable freelance business.

OVERCOMING LONELINESS AS A FREELANCER

Introduction

Freelancing offers many benefits, such as flexibility and the ability to work from anywhere. However, one of the challenges freelancers often face is loneliness. Working independently can sometimes lead to feelings of isolation, which can impact your mental health and productivity. This bonus chapter provides strategies to help you stay connected and overcome loneliness as a freelancer.

Understanding the Loneliness of Freelancing

Nature of Freelancing:

Remote Work: Freelancers often work from home or in isolated environments, reducing face-to-face interactions with colleagues.

Lack of Team Dynamics: Unlike traditional office jobs, freelancers typically don't have a built-in team for daily social interactions and support.

Psychological Impact:

Isolation: Prolonged periods of working alone can lead to feelings of isolation and disconnection.

Motivation: Loneliness can affect your motivation and energy levels, making it harder to stay productive.

Strategies to Combat Loneliness

Create a Social Routine:

Regular Check-Ins: Schedule regular check-ins with friends, family, or fellow freelancers. This can be through video calls, phone calls, or in-person meetings.

Join Online Communities: Participate in online forums, social media groups, or Slack communities related to your industry. Engaging in discussions and networking can help you feel connected.

Co-Working Spaces:

Membership: Consider joining a co-working space where you can work alongside other professionals. These spaces offer opportunities for social interaction and networking.

Events and Workshops: Many co-working spaces host events, workshops, and social gatherings. Participate in these activities to meet new people and build a sense of community.

Professional Networking:

Industry Events: Attend industry conferences, meetups, and networking events. These gatherings provide opportunities to meet like-minded professionals and potential collaborators.

Local Meetups: Look for local meetups or professional groups in your area. Websites like Meetup.com can help you find events relevant to your interests.

Collaborate with Other Freelancers:

Joint Projects: Partner with other freelancers on projects. Collaboration can provide social interaction and a sense of teamwork.

Peer Support Groups: Form or join peer support groups where freelancers can share experiences, challenges, and advice.

Establish a Work-Life Balance:

Set Boundaries: Create clear boundaries between work and personal time. Ensure you have time for social activities and relaxation.

Regular Breaks: Take regular breaks throughout the day to recharge and avoid burnout. Use this time to step outside, exercise, or connect with others.

Engage in Hobbies and Interests:

Pursue Passions: Engage in hobbies and activities that you enjoy outside of work. Join clubs or groups related to your interests to meet new people.

Volunteer Work: Consider volunteering for local organizations or causes you care about. Volunteering can provide a sense of purpose and community involvement.

Leveraging Technology for Connection

Communication Tools:

Video Calls: Use video call platforms like Zoom, Skype, or Google Meet for face-to-face interactions with clients, colleagues, and friends.

Instant Messaging: Stay connected with colleagues and peers through instant messaging apps like Slack, WhatsApp, or Telegram.

Virtual Co-Working:

Virtual Co-Working Sessions: Join or create virtual co-working sessions where you work alongside others via video call. Platforms like Focusmate facilitate these sessions.

Accountability Partners: Partner with another freelancer to set goals and check in regularly. This can provide motivation and a sense of camaraderie.

Online Learning and Workshops:

Webinars and Courses: Participate in online webinars and courses to learn new skills and interact with fellow learners.

Interactive Sessions: Choose interactive sessions that include group discussions and networking opportunities.

Case Studies: Freelancers Overcoming Loneliness

Case Study 1: The Social Networker:

Scenario: Alex, a freelance graphic designer, felt isolated working from home. He joined several online design communities and started attending local design meetups.

Outcome: Alex built a strong network of peers, gained new clients through referrals, and felt more connected to the design community.

Case Study 2: The Co-Working Advocate:

Scenario: Maria, a freelance writer, joined a co-working space to combat loneliness. She participated in social events and collaborated with other freelancers on joint projects.

Outcome: Maria formed meaningful professional relationships, increased her productivity, and enjoyed a better work-life balance.

Case Study 3: The Virtual Collaborator:

Scenario: John, a freelance web developer, set up virtual co-working sessions with other developers. They shared goals, provided feedback, and supported each other.

Outcome: John felt less isolated, improved his skills through peer feedback, and completed projects more efficiently.

Conclusion

Loneliness is a common challenge for freelancers, but it can be effectively managed with proactive strategies. By creating a social routine, leveraging co-working spaces, engaging in professional networking, collaborating with other freelancers, and using technology to stay connected, you can overcome isolation and thrive as a freelancer.

Remember, building a support network and maintaining a healthy work-life balance are key to sustaining your freelance career and overall well-being.

This chapter on overcoming loneliness as a freelancer provides practical tips and strategies to help you stay connected and maintain your mental health. By implementing these suggestions, you can create a fulfilling and socially enriched freelance experience. Happy freelancing!

SCALING YOUR FREELANCE BUSINESS

Expanding Your Service Offerings

Scaling your freelance business often starts with expanding the range of services you offer. Diversifying your services can attract a broader client base and increase your income potential.

Identifying New Opportunities:

Market Research: Conduct research to identify emerging trends and demands in your industry. Stay informed about new technologies and methodologies that can enhance your services.

Client Feedback: Listen to your clients' needs and challenges. They can provide valuable insights into additional services they might require.

Adding Complementary Services:

Skill Diversification: Consider upskilling or learning new skills that complement your current offerings. For example, a graphic designer might learn web development to offer complete website solutions.

Service Bundling: Bundle related services into packages. For instance, a digital marketer could offer SEO, content creation, and social media management as a comprehensive marketing package.

Testing New Services:

Pilot Projects: Launch new services with a few select clients to test their viability and gather feedback. This allows you to refine the service before offering it to a broader audience.

Promotional Offers: Introduce new services at a discounted rate or with added value to attract initial clients and build a portfolio.

Hiring Subcontractors

As your business grows, you may need to bring in additional help to manage the increased workload. Hiring subcontractors can allow you to take on larger projects and scale your operations.

Finding and Managing Subcontractors:

Recruitment: Use freelance platforms, industry forums, and your professional network to find qualified subcontractors. Look for individuals with complementary skills and a proven track record.

Onboarding: Develop an onboarding process to familiarize subcontractors with your workflows, tools, and quality standards. Clear communication and expectations are key to successful collaboration.

Legal Considerations and Agreements:

Contracts: Draft detailed contracts that outline the scope of work, payment terms, confidentiality agreements, and intellectual property rights. Ensure that your subcontractors understand and agree to these terms.

Non-Disclosure Agreements (NDAs): Use NDAs to protect sensitive client information and your proprietary processes.

Quality Control:

Supervision: Regularly review the work of your subcontractors to ensure it meets your standards. Provide constructive feedback and support to help them improve.

Client Communication: Maintain direct communication with your clients. While subcontractors may handle the execution, you should remain the primary point of contact to manage expectations and address any concerns.

Automation and Efficiency

Leveraging automation tools can significantly improve your efficiency, allowing you to handle more clients and projects without sacrificing quality.

Tools for Automating Your Workflow:

Project Management: Use tools like Asana, Trello, or Monday.com to manage tasks, deadlines, and team collaboration.

Client Relationship Management (CRM): Implement CRM systems like HubSpot or Salesforce to streamline client communications, manage leads, and track project statuses.

Invoicing and Payments: Automate invoicing and payment processing with tools like FreshBooks, QuickBooks, or Wave. These tools can also help with expense tracking and financial reporting.

Time Management Techniques:

Time Blocking: Allocate specific blocks of time for different tasks to ensure focused and efficient work periods. Tools like Google Calendar or TimeBloc can help with scheduling.

Pomodoro Technique: Use the Pomodoro Technique to break work into intervals (typically 25 minutes), followed by short breaks. This can enhance productivity and reduce burnout.

Task Prioritization: Prioritize tasks based on their importance and deadlines. The Eisenhower Matrix (categorizing tasks as urgent/important) can help with effective prioritization.

Case Studies: Scaling Your Freelance Business

Learning from the experiences of other freelancers who have successfully scaled their businesses can provide practical insights and inspiration.

Case Study 1: Expanding Service Offerings:

Scenario: A freelance content writer expanded their services to include SEO consulting and content strategy. By offering a comprehensive package, they attracted larger clients looking for end-to-end solutions.

Outcome: The freelancer's revenue increased by 40%, and they secured long-term contracts with multiple clients.

Case Study 2: Hiring Subcontractors:

Scenario: A freelance web developer started receiving more projects than they could handle. They hired a team of subcontractors, including designers and junior developers, to assist with various aspects of the projects.

Outcome: The freelancer was able to take on larger projects, resulting in a 50% increase in annual income and the ability to handle multiple high-profile clients simultaneously.

Case Study 3: Implementing Automation:

Scenario: A freelance marketer struggled with managing multiple clients and administrative tasks. They implemented automation tools for email marketing, project management, and invoicing.

Outcome: The marketer saved over 10 hours per week on administrative tasks, allowing them to focus on strategic work and client acquisition, leading to a 30% growth in their client base.

Future-Proofing Your Business

As the freelance landscape continues to evolve, it's important to stay ahead of the curve and future-proof your business.

Adapting to Market Changes:

Continuous Learning: Stay updated with industry trends, new technologies, and best practices. Invest in continuous learning through courses, webinars, and professional development.

Flexibility: Be prepared to adapt your services and business model to meet changing market demands and client needs.

Building a Strong Network:

Professional Associations: Join professional associations and networking groups in your industry. These organizations can provide valuable resources, support, and opportunities for collaboration.

Mentorship: Seek mentorship from experienced freelancers or business professionals who can offer guidance and advice as you scale your business.

Diversifying Income Streams:

Passive Income: Explore passive income opportunities such as creating and selling digital products, online courses, or writing eBooks.

Multiple Clients: Avoid relying too heavily on a single client. Diversify your client base to ensure a stable and resilient income stream.

Scaling your freelance business requires strategic planning, effective management, and a willingness to adapt and grow. By expanding your services, hiring subcontractors, leveraging automation, and learning from successful case studies, you can take your freelance business to new heights.

The next chapter will explore the future of global freelancing, emerging trends, and how to prepare for the opportunities and challenges ahead.

MAINTAINING GOOD CLIENT RELATIONSHIPS AS A FREELANCER

Introduction

Building and maintaining good client relationships is vital for long-term success as a freelancer. Strong client relationships lead to repeat business, referrals, and a positive reputation in your industry. This chapter provides strategies and best practices for nurturing and sustaining productive and professional relationships with your clients.

Step 1: Set Clear Expectations

Detailed Contracts:

Always use a detailed contract that outlines the scope of work, deliverables, timelines, payment terms, and any other relevant details. This helps prevent misunderstandings and sets a professional tone from the start.

Clear Communication:

Clearly communicate your availability, preferred communication methods, and expected response times. This helps manage client expectations and reduces the likelihood of misunderstandings.

Project Kickoff Meetings:

Hold a kickoff meeting at the start of each project to discuss goals, expectations, and any specific requirements. This ensures that both you and the client are on the same page.

Step 2: Communicate Regularly and Effectively

Regular Updates:

Provide regular updates on the progress of the project. This can be done through weekly emails, progress reports, or scheduled meetings.

Responsive Communication:

Respond to client inquiries promptly. Timely responses demonstrate professionalism and respect for the client's time.

Transparency:

Be transparent about any challenges or delays that may arise. Clients appreciate honesty and are more likely to be understanding if issues are communicated early.

Step 3: Deliver Quality Work

Attention to Detail:

Pay close attention to the details of your work to ensure high quality. Double-check your work for errors and make sure it meets or exceeds client expectations.

Consistency:

Maintain a consistent level of quality in all your work. Consistency builds trust and reliability, making clients more likely to return for future projects.

Exceed Expectations:

Whenever possible, go above and beyond to exceed client expectations. This could be through delivering early, providing extra value, or offering insights and suggestions.

Step 4: Handle Feedback and Revisions Professionally

Open to Feedback:

Be open to feedback and view it as an opportunity for improvement. Listen to the client's concerns and suggestions without becoming defensive.

Revisions:

Handle revisions professionally and promptly. Clearly outline your revision policy in the initial contract to manage expectations regarding the number and scope of revisions.

Constructive Criticism:

Use constructive criticism to enhance your skills and deliver better results in the future. Reflect on feedback and apply it to improve your work.

Step 5: Build Trust and Rapport

Personal Connection:

Take the time to build a personal connection with your clients. Remember details about their preferences, interests, and important milestones.

Reliability:

Be reliable and dependable. Meet deadlines, follow through on promises, and be consistent in your communication and work quality.

Professionalism:

Maintain a high level of professionalism in all your interactions. This includes being polite, respectful, and maintaining boundaries.

Step 6: Show Appreciation

Thank You Notes:

Send thank you notes or emails after completing a project to show your appreciation for the client's business.

Client Gifts:

Consider sending small, thoughtful gifts to long-term clients during the holidays or after a significant project. This gesture can strengthen your relationship.

Referral Incentives:

Offer referral incentives to clients who refer new business to you. This not only shows appreciation but also encourages clients to spread the word about your services.

Step 7: Foster Long-Term Relationships

Follow-Up:

Follow up with clients after project completion to ensure they are satisfied with the work and to keep the lines of communication open for future projects.

Ongoing Support:

Offer ongoing support and maintenance services if applicable. This can provide additional value to the client and create opportunities for repeat business.

Stay in Touch:

Keep in touch with past clients through regular check-ins, newsletters, or sharing relevant content. Staying top-of-mind increases the likelihood of future collaborations.

Step 8: Manage Difficult Situations Gracefully

Conflict Resolution:

Approach conflicts or disagreements calmly and professionally. Listen to the client's perspective, address their concerns, and work towards a mutually beneficial resolution.

Problem-Solving:

Be proactive in solving problems that arise during a project. Demonstrating your problem-solving skills can build trust and confidence in your abilities.

Learn and Improve:

Reflect on difficult situations and learn from them. Use these experiences to improve your processes and communication for future projects.

Conclusion

Maintaining good client relationships is essential for a successful freelance career.

By setting clear expectations, communicating regularly, delivering quality work, handling feedback professionally, building trust, showing appreciation, fostering long-term relationships, and managing difficult situations gracefully, you can create a strong foundation for lasting and productive client relationships. These efforts not only lead to repeat business and referrals but also contribute to a positive reputation in your industry.

This chapter on maintaining good client relationships as a freelancer provides practical strategies and best practices to help you build and sustain strong, professional connections with your clients. By prioritizing these relationships, you can enhance your business success and enjoy a more fulfilling freelance career.

CASE STUDIES AND SUCCESS STORIES

Introduction

Learning from the experiences of others can provide invaluable insights and inspiration for your own freelance journey. This chapter presents a collection of case studies and success stories from freelancers who have excelled in various fields. These real-world examples highlight the challenges they faced, the strategies they employed, and the outcomes they achieved.

Case Study 1: The Creative Designer

Background:

Maria, a graphic designer based in Brazil, decided to expand her freelance business internationally. She had a strong portfolio but limited experience with global clients.

Challenges:

Navigating language barriers and cultural differences. Building a global clientele from a local base.

Managing time zones effectively.

Strategies:

Online Presence: Maria revamped her website to appeal to an international audience. She included an English version and optimized it for search engines to attract global clients.

Freelance Platforms: She joined platforms like Upwork and Behance, where she showcased her work and bid on international projects.

Networking: Maria attended virtual design conferences and joined international design communities on LinkedIn and Facebook.

Outcome:

Maria secured clients from the US, UK, and Australia, significantly increasing her income.

She built long-term relationships with several international clients who provided consistent work.

Maria's portfolio now includes diverse projects that enhance her credibility and attract more global opportunities.

Case Study 2: The Tech Consultant

Background:

John, a freelance IT consultant from Canada, aimed to leverage his expertise in cybersecurity to attract high-profile clients globally.

Challenges:

Competing with established firms and consultants worldwide.

Ensuring compliance with different countries' cybersecurity regulations.

Building trust with international clients.

Strategies:

Certifications and Expertise: John obtained internationally recognized certifications (CISSP, CISM) to bolster his credentials.

Content Marketing: He started a blog and a YouTube channel where he shared cybersecurity insights, tutorials, and case studies, establishing himself as an authority in the field.

Client Education: John offered free webinars and workshops on cybersecurity best practices, which helped build trust and showcase his expertise.

Outcome:

John landed contracts with multinational corporations, including a major financial institution.

His content marketing efforts attracted a steady stream of inquiries, leading to more projects.

John's business grew by 60% within a year, allowing him to hire a small team of subcontractors.

Case Study 3: The Digital Marketer

Background:

Emma, a digital marketer from the UK, wanted to specialize in social media marketing for the fashion industry. She aimed to become a go-to expert for fashion brands globally.

Challenges:

Differentiating herself in a saturated market.
Understanding and adapting to different cultural preferences in fashion.
Scaling her business without compromising quality.

Strategies:

Niche Focus: Emma focused exclusively on the fashion industry, developing deep expertise and creating tailored marketing strategies for fashion brands.

Visual Portfolio: She built a visually stunning portfolio on Instagram and Pinterest, showcasing her work with various fashion brands.

Client Testimonials and Case Studies: Emma collected detailed testimonials and created case studies highlighting the results she achieved for her clients.

Outcome:

Emma became a sought-after digital marketer in the fashion industry, working with brands from Europe, Asia, and North America.

Her revenue doubled within 18 months, and she was able to hire assistants to manage the increased workload.

Emma's reputation as a fashion marketing expert grew, leading to speaking engagements and collaborations with top industry influencers.

Success Stories: Interviews with Top Freelancers

Interview 1: Michael, the Software Developer

Question: What was your biggest challenge in going global, and how did you overcome it?

Michael: "The biggest challenge was building trust with clients who had never met me in person. I overcame this by consistently delivering high-quality work and being transparent in my communication. Regular updates, video calls, and detailed reports helped build that trust."

Interview 2: Sarah, the Content Writer

Question: What strategies helped you scale your freelance business?

Sarah: "Networking and referrals were key. I made it a point to attend industry conferences and join professional associations. Providing exceptional service led to word-of-mouth referrals, which significantly boosted my business."

Interview 3: Raj, the Virtual Assistant

Question: How do you manage working with clients across different time zones?

Raj: "I use scheduling tools to manage my time effectively. I set clear expectations with clients about my working hours and always strive to be flexible. Using shared calendars and communication tools like Slack and Trello has been a game-changer."

Lessons Learned from Success Stories

Consistency and Quality: Delivering consistent, high-quality work is crucial for building a reputation and securing long-term clients.

Adaptability: Being adaptable to different cultures, time zones, and client preferences can significantly enhance your global freelancing success.

Networking: Building and leveraging a strong professional network can open doors to new opportunities and provide valuable support.

Specialization: Focusing on a niche or industry can help you stand out in a crowded market and become a go-to expert.

Client Relationships: Maintaining strong relationships with clients through clear communication, transparency, and excellent customer service is essential for long-term success.

By studying these case studies and success stories, you can gain practical insights and strategies to apply to your own freelance business.

The experiences of successful freelancers demonstrate that with the right approach, you can overcome challenges and achieve remarkable success on a global scale.

The final chapter will explore the future of global freelancing, emerging trends, and how to prepare for the opportunities and challenges ahead.

THE FUTURE OF GLOBAL FREELANCING

Emerging Trends

The landscape of freelancing is continually evolving, driven by technological advancements, changing economic conditions, and shifting cultural attitudes toward work. Here are some emerging trends that are shaping the future of global freelancing:

Remote Work Normalization:

Post-Pandemic Shift: The COVID-19 pandemic accelerated the adoption of remote work, a trend that is likely to continue. Companies have realized the benefits of a remote workforce, leading to increased opportunities for freelancers.

Hybrid Work Models: Many organizations are adopting hybrid work models, blending remote and in-office work. This shift opens up more freelance opportunities as companies look for flexible, on-demand talent.

AI and Automation:

Enhanced Efficiency: Automation tools and AI are making it easier for freelancers to manage administrative tasks, freeing up more time for creative and strategic work.

New Opportunities: AI and machine learning are creating new fields and opportunities for freelancers, particularly in data analysis, machine learning development, and AI integration.

Gig Economy Growth:

Platform Expansion: Freelance platforms are expanding their services, offering more tools and resources to help freelancers succeed. These platforms are also becoming more specialized, catering to niche markets.

Increased Competition: As the gig economy grows, competition among freelancers is intensifying. Differentiation and specialization are becoming more important for standing out.

Global Collaboration:

Cross-Border Teams: Advances in communication and collaboration tools are enabling freelancers to work seamlessly with clients and teams across the globe.

Cultural Exchange: Increased global collaboration is leading to a richer exchange of ideas and cultural perspectives, enhancing creativity and innovation.

Opportunities and Challenges

While the future of global freelancing is bright, it comes with its own set of opportunities and challenges. Understanding these can help you prepare and adapt to the changing landscape.

Opportunities:

Access to Global Markets: Freelancers can tap into a global market, offering services to clients in different countries and industries.

Diverse Work: Exposure to diverse projects and clients enhances your skills and broadens your experience.

Higher Earnings Potential: With access to international clients, freelancers can often command higher rates, especially in specialized fields.

Challenges:

Competition: The growing number of freelancers means increased competition. It's crucial to differentiate yourself through expertise, quality, and unique value propositions.

Regulatory Hurdles: Navigating different countries' legal and tax requirements can be complex. Freelancers need to stay informed about international regulations.

Cultural Differences: Understanding and adapting to cultural differences in communication and work styles is essential for successful international collaborations.

Preparing for the Future

To thrive in the evolving landscape of global freelancing, you need to be proactive and strategic. Here's how to prepare for the future:

Continuous Learning:

Stay Updated: Keep abreast of industry trends, technological advancements, and market demands. Regularly update your skills through courses, certifications, and professional development.

Adaptability: Be open to learning new tools and techniques. Adaptability will help you stay relevant and competitive.

Building a Strong Network:

Professional Associations: Join professional associations and networking groups relevant to your industry. These organizations provide valuable resources, support, and networking opportunities.

Online Presence: Maintain a strong online presence through social media, professional platforms, and personal websites. Engage with your network regularly to build relationships and attract opportunities.

Diversifying Income Streams:

Passive Income: Explore passive income opportunities such as creating and selling digital products, online courses, or writing eBooks.

Multiple Clients: Avoid relying too heavily on a single client. Diversify your client base to ensure a stable and resilient income stream.

Embracing Technology:

Automation Tools: Utilize automation tools to streamline your workflow and improve efficiency. This allows you to focus on high-value tasks and projects.

Collaboration Platforms: Use collaboration platforms to enhance communication and project management with clients and team members. Tools like Slack, Trello, and Asana can facilitate smooth operations.

Vision for the Future

As we look to the future, the potential for global freelancing is immense. Here are some visions for what the future might hold:

Freelance Ecosystem: A robust ecosystem of freelancers, clients, platforms, and support services that fosters collaboration, innovation, and growth.

Skill-Based Economy: An economy that values skills and expertise over traditional employment structures, offering greater opportunities for freelancers.

Global Community: A vibrant global community of freelancers who share knowledge, support each other, and collaborate on impactful projects.

Conclusion

The future of global freelancing is full of possibilities. By staying informed, adapting to changes, and leveraging new opportunities, you can position yourself for long-term success. Embrace the challenges, celebrate the successes, and continue to grow as a global freelancer.

Final Thoughts:

Remember, the journey of a freelancer is dynamic and ever-evolving. Stay curious, be proactive, and always strive for excellence. Your ability to adapt and innovate will be your greatest asset in navigating the future of global freelancing.

This concludes "The Global Freelancer: Finding Clients and Projects Anywhere." May this book serve as your guide, inspiration, and roadmap to a successful and fulfilling freelance career on the global stage.

THE END

Please leave a review.

ABOUT THE AUTHOR

Genevieve Velzian

Genevieve Velzian is a full time digital nomad and traveller, who has visited 40 countries and counting. As well as running successful freelance data strategy gigs, she has various other income streams and meets fascinating entrepreneurs on her travels. She believes strongly in creating a personal brand, and becoming a Key Person of Influence during a freelance journey.